THE BOOSEY & HAWKES MASTERWORKS LIBRARY

AARON COPLAND

ORCHESTRAL ANTHOLOGY · *Volume 2*

ANTHOLOGIE D'ŒUVRES POUR ORCHESTRE • VOLUME 2
ANTHOLOGIE VON ORCHESTERWERKEN • BAND 2

Quiet City
Lincoln Portrait
Danzón Cubano
Clarinet Concerto
Three Latin-American Sketches

BOOSEY & HAWKES

London · New York · Berlin · Sydney

Publisher's note
The publishers have used their best efforts to clear the copyright for images used in this volume with the relevant owners and print suitable acknowledgements. If any copyright owner has not been consulted or an acknowledgement has been omitted, the publishers offer their apologies and will rectify the situation following formal notification.

Cover design by Lynette Williamson
Front cover picture: *Sunday in New England* by Jane Wooster Scott (20th century) David David Gallery, Philadelphia, PA, USA/Bridgeman Art Library, London/ New York
Preface © Copyright 1999 by Malcolm MacDonald
Printed and bound in England by Halstan & Co. Ltd, Amersham, Bucks.

Contents

Preface

This anthology of Aaron Copland's orchestral works, like its companion, *Orchestral Anthology Volume 1*, illustrates his ability to illuminate aspects, atmospheres, musical idioms and historical associations of both North and South America while always remaining true to his personal style of writing.

Quiet City originated in 1939 as part of Copland's incidental music to the play of the same title by Irwin Shaw. In 1940 he recast it for string orchestra with solo trumpet and cor anglais. In form and character it is a lyric nocturne, evoking a sleeping, deserted urban landscape with a reticent poetry that has made it one of its composer's best-loved short pieces.

Shortly after America's entry into World War II, the conductor Andre Kostelanetz asked several prominent American composers to create a 'portrait gallery' of great Americans. Copland originally chose Walt Whitman, but when Kostelanetz asked him to write a piece about a statesman he immediately focused upon Abraham Lincoln. Premiered in Cincinnati in May 1942, with Kostelanetz conducting and William Adams speaking the text (which is drawn almost exclusively from Lincoln's great Civil War speeches), *Lincoln Portrait* is one of the relatively few successful works to combine music and the spoken word. Copland's score incorporates phrases from popular tunes of the Civil War era, such as 'The Camptown Races' at the climax of the extended orchestral introduction, and the main theme of the piece derives from the folksong 'On Springfield Mountain'.

Danzón Cubano was originally a work for two pianos, which Copland and Leonard Bernstein performed for the first time in December 1942. The orchestral arrangement was premiered in Baltimore in February 1946; the following year it gained the New York Music Critics' Circle Award. The *danzón* is a Cuban traditional dance in two parts, the first elegant and restrained and the second much livelier, but the whole poised and aristocratic in expression. Although the piece incorporates melodic and rhythmic fragments Copland had heard during several visits to Cuba, he was careful to point out that it was not an authentic *danzón* but 'only an American tourist's impression' of the traditional dance.

The Clarinet Concerto was commissioned by the jazz clarinettist Benny Goodman and written in South America and New York State during 1947-8. Copland here pits the solo wind instrument against a particularly transparent ensemble of bowed, plucked and struck strings: string orchestra, harp and piano. The work is also a homage to the playing style of Goodman, known world-wide at the time as the 'King of Swing'. Although Goodman was initially nonplussed by the demands of the solo part, he gave the world premiere (on 6 November 1950 with the NBC Symphony Orchestra under Fritz Reiner) and went on to make this one of the most renowned of modern clarinet concerti. Like Copland's Piano Concerto of 20 years earlier, the work is cast in two movements - one mainly slow, the other mainly fast - played without a break, connected by a cadenza for the soloist.

Of the *Three Latin-American Sketches* - comprising 'Estribillo', a lively piece on Venezuelan popular materials, and two Mexican pieces, a lyrical landscape ('Paisaje Mexicano') and bouncy dance - Copland commented: 'The tunes, the rhythms and the temperament . . . are folksy, while the orchestration is bright and snappy and the music sizzles along'. These were his last essays in Latin-American style. He composed the Mexican movements at Acapulco in 1959: the 'Danza de Jalisco' was premiered in Spoleto, Italy, that year and in 1965 Copland conducted both movements, under the title *Two Mexican Pieces*, at a private concert of the Pan-American Union in Washington. He then withdrew them as too short to be effective, but in 1971, at the suggestion of Andre Kostelanetz, he composed the Venezuelan piece 'Estribillo' and revised the 'Danza' to complete the triptych, which Kostelanetz premiered with the New York Philharmonic in June 1972.

Malcolm MacDonald

Préface

Cette anthologie des œuvres orchestrales d'Aaron Copland tout comme *Anthologie d'Œuvres pour Orchestre Volume 1,* illustre ses capacités à illuminer des aspects, des atmosphères, des langages musicaux et des associations historiques des deux Amériques tout en restant fidèle à son style d'écriture personnel.

Quiet City (Ville Tranquille) provient de la musique de scène que Copland écrivit en 1939 pour la pièce d'Irwin Shaw qui porte ce titre. En 1940, il la réorchestra pour orchestre à cordes, trompette solo et cor anglais. De forme et de caractère c'est un nocturne lyrique qui évoque un paysage urbain somnolent, désert, avec une poésie réticente qui en fait l'une des plus appréciées parmi les œuvres courtes du compositeur.

Peu après l'entrée des Etats-Unis dans la seconde guerre mondiale le chef d'orchestre André Kostelanetz demanda à plusieurs compositeurs américains de premier plan de créer une « galerie de portraits » de grands personnages américains. Copland choisit d'abord Walt Whitman, mais lorsque Kostalenetz lui demanda de prendre un homme d'état comme sujet, il choisit immédiatement Abraham Lincoln. Créé à Cincinnati en mai 1942, sous la direction de Kostelanetz et avec William Adams comme récitant (le texte est tiré presque exclusivement des grands discours de Lincoln durant la Guerre de Sécession), *Lincoln Portrait* (Portrait de Lincoln) est une des rares œuvres à associer musique et texte parlé avec succès. La partition de Copland inclut des phrases tirées d'airs populaires de la Guerre de Sécession tels que «The Camptown Races » (Les courses de Camptown) au point culminant de la longue introduction orchestrale, et le principal thème de l'œuvre est dérivé de la chanson traditionnelle « On Springfield Mountain » (Sur le Mont Springfield).

Danzón Cubano fut d'abord une œuvre pour deux pianos, que Copland est Leonard Bernstein jouèrent pour la première fois en décembre 1942. La création de la version pour orchestre eut lieu à Baltimore en février 1946 ; l'année suivante, elle remporta le prix du Cercle des Critiques Musicaux de New York. Le *danzón* est une danse cubaine traditionnelle en deux parties, la première élégante et retenue, et la seconde plus animée, mais le tout dans une expression posée et aristocratique. Quoique cette œuvre comporte des fragments mélodiques et rythmiques que Copland avait entendus lors de ses séjours à Cuba, il prenait soin de souligner qu'il ne s'agissait pas là d'un authentique *danzón* mais « simplement une impression de touriste américain » de la danse traditionnelle.

Le Concerto pour Clarinette fut commandé par le clarinettiste de jazz Benny Goodman et composé en Amérique du Sud et dans l'état de New York durant 1947-8. Ici Copland place les instruments à vent solistes en face d'un ensemble particulièrement transparent de cordes frottées, pincées et frappées : orchestre à cordes, harpe et piano. L'œuvre est également un hommage rendu au style de Benny Goodman, connu à l'époque dans le monde entier comme « le roi du swing ». Quoique de prime abord Goodman était déconcerté par les difficultés de la partie soliste, il en donna la première mondiale (le 6 novembre 1950 avec le NBC Symphony Orchestra sous la direction de Fritz Reiner) et en fit par la suite l'un des concerti modernes pour clarinette les plus renommés. Tout comme le Concerto pour Piano de Copland quelque vingt ans auparavant, cette œuvre comporte deux mouvements - le premier lent pour l'essentiel, le second plutôt rapide - joués sans interruption, reliés l'un à l'autre par une cadence du soliste.

A propos des *Three Latin-American Sketches* (Trois Esquisses Latino-Américaines), qui comprennent « Estribillo », morceau animé sur un matériau populaire vénézuélien, et de deux morceaux mexicains, un paysage lyrique « Paisaje Mexicano » et une danse enjouée, Copland déclara : « Les airs, les rythmes et le tempérament . . . sont folkloriques, tandis que l'orchestration est brillante et vive, et la musique pétille. » Ce furent ses derniers essais dans le style latino-américain. Il composa les mouvements mexicains à Acapulco en 1959 ; la « Danza de Jalisco » fut créée à Spoleto en Italie cette même année et en 1965 Copland dirigea les deux mouvements, sous le titre *Two Mexican Pieces* (Deux Morceaux Mexicains) lors d'un concert privé de la Pan-American Union à Washington. Il les retira ensuite, les jugeant trop courts pour être vraiment efficaces, mais en 1971, sur la suggestion d'André Kostelanetz, il composa le mouvement vénézuélien « Estribillo » et révisa la « Danza » pour compléter ce triptyque, dont Kostelanetz dirigea la création avec le New York Philharmonic en juin 1972.

Malcolm MacDonald

Vorwort

Diese Anthologie mit Orchesterwerken Aaron Coplands zeigt, ebenso wie bereits die *Anthologie von Orchesterwerken Band 1*, die Fähigkeit des Komponisten, verschiedene Aspekte, Stimmungen, musikalische Idiome und historische Assoziationen Nord- und Südamerikas aufscheinen zu lassen und sich dennoch eine ganz eigene Musiksprache zu bewahren.

Quiet City entstand 1939 als Teil von Coplands Bühnenmusik zu Irwin Shaws gleichnamigen Schauspiel. 1940 arbeitete er es für Streichorchester mit Solotrompete und Englischhorn um. Form und Charakter weisen es als lyrisches Nocturne aus, das die Vorstellung einer schlafenden oder verlassenen urbanen Landschaft evoziert und dessen leise Poesie es zu einem der beliebtesten, kürzeren Werke Coplands gemacht hat.

Kurz nach Amerikas Eintritt in den Zweiten Weltkrieg bat der Dirigent Andre Kostelanetz mehrere prominente amerikanische Komponisten eine ‚Portrait-Galerie‘ großer Amerikaner zu schaffen. Copland wählte ursprünglich Walt Whitman, entschied sich dann aber für Abraham Lincoln, nachdem Kostelanetz ihm ein Stück über einen Staatsmann nahegelegt hatte. Die Uraufführung fand im Mai 1942 in Cincinnati statt: Kostelanetz dirigierte, William Adams sprach den Text, der fast ausschließlich Lincolns großen Bürgerkriegsreden entnommen war. *Lincoln Portrait* ist eines der verhältnismäßig wenigen Stücke, denen es gelingt, Musik und gesprochenes Wort überzeugend zu verbinden. Copland hat in seine Partitur populäre Melodien der Bürgerkriegszeit eingebunden wie ‚The Camptown Races‘, die auf dem Höhepunkt der ausgedehnten Orchestereinleitung erklingt. Das Hauptthema des Werkes ist eine Ableitung des Volkslieds ‚On Springfield Mountain‘.

Danzón Cubano war ursprünglich ein Werk für zwei Klaviere, das von Copland und Leonard Bernstein im Dezember 1942 uraufgeführt wurde. Die Orchesterfassung erklang erstmals in Baltimore Februar 1946; ein Jahr später wurde es mit dem New York Music Critics' Circle Award ausgezeichnet. Bei einem *Danzón* handelt es sich um einen zweiteiligen, traditionellen kubanischen Tanz. Er beginnt im ersten Teil elegant und zurückhaltend, wird im zweiten sehr viel lebhafter, bewahrt sich aber insgesamt Gleichmaß und Aristokratie im Ausdruck. Wenn das Stück auch melodische und rhythmische Höreindrücke verwendet, die Copland während seiner häufigen Reisen in Kuba in sich aufgenommen hatte, wies er ausdrücklich darauf hin, daß es sich bei seinem Werk nicht um einen authentischen *Danzón* handele, sondern es lediglich den Eindruck wiedergebe, den dieser traditionelle Tanz auf einen amerikanischen Touristen ausgeübt habe.

Der Jazzklarinettist Benny Goodman bat Copland um ein Klarinettenkonzert. Copland schrieb es in Südamerika und New York 1947/48. Er kontrastiert hier das Soloinstrument mit einem besonders transparent besetzten Ensemble, bestehend aus Streich-, Zupf- und Tasteninstrumenten: Streichorchester, Harfe und Klavier. Das Werk ist auch eine Hommage an die Spieltechnik Goodmans, der als ‚King of Swing‘ Weltruhm genoß. War er zunächst auch verblüfft über die Anforderungen, die der Solopart an ihn stellte, spielte er die Welturaufführung am 6. November 1950 mit dem NBC Symphony Orchestra unter Fritz Reiner und machte aus diesem Werk eines der berühmtesten Klarinettenkonzerte des 20. Jahrhunderts. Wie das 20 Jahre ältere Klavierkonzert besteht auch das Klarinettenkonzert aus zwei Sätzen, einem überwiegend langsamen und einem eher schnellen Satz, die ohne Unterbrechung, aber mit überleitender Solokadenz gespielt werden.

Über die *Three Latin-American Sketches*, bestehend aus ‚Estribillo‘ - ein lebhaftes Stück auf der Grundlage populärer venezolanischer Musik - und zwei mexikanischen Stücken, einer lyrischen Landschaftsschilderung - ‚Paisaje Mexicano‘ - und ‚Danza de Jalisco‘, schrieb Copland: „Die Melodien, die Rhythmen und die Stimmung sind volkstümlich, die Orchestration ist durchsichtig und hell und die Musik sprüht Funken." Es sind seine letzten Arbeiten im lateinamerikanischen Stil. Die beiden mexikanisch inspirierten Stücke komponierte er 1959 in Acapulco: ‚Danza de Jalisco‘ wurde im selben Jahr in Spoleto (Italien) uraufgeführt. Beide Sätze unter dem Titel *Two Mexican Pieces* dirigierte Copland selbst bei einer geschlossenen Vorstellung der Pan-American Union in Washington 1965. Er zog sie schließlich zurück, da er sie für zu kurz hielt, um effektvoll zu sein. 1971 aber komponierte er auf Anregung von Andre Kostolanetz das venezolanische Stück ‚Estribillo‘ und überarbeitete ‚Danza‘, um das Triptychon zu vervollständigen, das Kostelanetz im Juni 1972 mit den New Yorker Philharmonikern uraufführte.

Malcolm MacDonald

QUIET CITY

Instrumentation

★English Horn or Oboe
Trumpet in B♭
Strings

★Use Oboe only if no English Horn is available.

To Ralph Hawkes

QUIET CITY

AARON COPLAND
(1940)

4

6

Poco più mosso (♩=54) (♩.=♩) (in 2)

12

14

*Exaggerated crescendo followed by a sudden piano

con sord.

mp (as at first)

15

Sept. '40
Lenox, Mass.
N.Y.C.

COPLAND 2000

LINCOLN PORTRAIT
For Narrator and Orchestra

Instrumentation

2 Flutes (doubling 2 Piccolos)
2 Oboes
★English Horn
2 Clarinets in B♭
★Bass Clarinet in B♭
2 Bassoons
★Contrabassoon
4 Horns in F
3 Trumpets in B♭ (★Trumpet 3)
3 Trombones
Tuba
Timpani
Percussion
snare drum, cymbals, bass drum, tam-tam,
glockenspiel, sleigh bells, xylophone
★Celeste
Harp
Strings

★These instruments are not essential to performance.

Duration: c. 14 minutes

Note for the Speaker

The speaker is cautioned against undue emphasis in the delivery of Lincoln's words. The words are sufficiently dramatic in themselves; they need no added "emotion" in order to put them across to an audience. They are meant to be read simply and directly, without a trace of exaggerated sentiment. It is the composer's wish that the Speaker depend for his effect, not on his "acting" ability, but on his complete sincerity of manner. How Lincoln spoke these words we can never really know, but certainly we can all sense how *not* to read them.

LINCOLN PORTRAIT

SPEAKER:

"Fellow citizens, we cannot escape history."

That is what he said,
That is what Abraham Lincoln said:

"Fellow citizens, we cannot escape history. We of this Congress and this administration will be remembered in spite of ourselves. No personal significance or insignificance can spare one or another of us. The fiery trial through which we pass will light us down, in honor or dishonor, to the latest generation. We - even we here - hold the power and bear the responsibility."

He was born in Kentucky, raised in Indiana, and lived in Illinois.
And this is what he said:
This is what Abe Lincoln said:
He said:

"The dogmas of the quiet past are inadequate to the stormy present. The occasion is piled high with difficulty, and we must rise with the occasion. As our case is new, so we must think anew and act anew. We must disenthrall ourselves, and then we shall save our country."

When standing erect he was six feet four inches tall.
And this is what he said:
He said:

"It is the eternal struggle between two principles - right and wrong - throughout the world . . . It is the same spirit that says 'You toil and work and earn bread - and I'll eat it.' No matter in what shape it comes, whether from the mouth of a king who seeks to bestride the people of his own nation and live by the fruit of their labor, or from one race of men as an apology for enslaving another race, it is the same tyrannical principle!"

Lincoln was a quiet man.
Abe Lincoln was a quiet and a melancholy man.
But when he spoke of democracy,
This is what he said:
He said:

"As I would not be a slave, so I would not be a master. This expresses my idea of democracy. Whatever differs from this, to the extent of the difference, is no democracy."

Abraham Lincoln, sixteenth President of the United States, is everlasting in the memory of his countrymen.
For on the battleground at Gettysburg, this is what he said:
He said:

". . . that from these honored dead we take increased devotion to that cause for which they gave the last full measure of devotion: that we here highly resolve that these dead shall not have died in vain; that this nation, under God, shall have a new birth of freedom; and that government of the people, and for the people, shall not perish from the earth."

Note

Cette traduction est fournie seulement comme référence, non pour la scène.

PORTRAIT DE LINCOLN

RECITANT:

« Chers concitoyens, nous ne pouvons pas échapper à l'histoire. »

Voilà ce qu'il a dit,
Voilà ce qu'Abraham Lincoln a dit :

« Chers concitoyens, nous ne pouvons pas échapper à l'histoire. Nous qui participons à ce Congrès et à cette administration resterons dans les mémoires malgré nous. L'importance ou le manque d'importance de l'un ou l'autre d'entre nous ne pourra pas l'en préserver. L'épreuve du feu à laquelle nous sommes soumis nous éclairera, dans l'honneur ou dans le déshonneur, jusqu'à la dernière génération. Nous - même nous ici présents - détenons le pouvoir et la responsabilité. »

Il était né dans le Kentucky, avait grandi dans l'Indiana, et vivait dans l'Illinois.
Et voici ce qu'il a dit :
Voici ce qu'Abraham Lincoln a dit :
Il a dit :

« Les dogmes du calme passé ne s'appliquent pas au tempétueux présent. L'heure est remplie de difficultés, et nous devons nous montrer digne de l'heure. Notre cas est nouveau, et nous devons penser de nouveau, et agir de nouveau. Nous devons sortir de notre torpeur, et alors nous sauverons notre pays. »

Quand il se tenait droit il mesurait 1 mètre 90.
Et voici ce qu'il a dit :
Il a dit :

« C'est la lutte éternelle entre deux principes - le bien et le mal - dans le monde entier . . . C'est le même esprit qui dit : « Tu peines, travailles, et gagnes ton pain - et c'est moi qui vais le manger. » Quelque soit la forme qu'il prend, que ce soit par la bouche d'un roi qui cherche à opprimer le peuple de sa propre nation et vivre des fruits de son labeur, ou comme prétexte d'une race d'hommes pour en réduire une autre en esclavage, c'est le même principe tyrannique ! »

Lincoln était un homme calme.
Abraham Lincoln était un homme calme et mélancolique. Mais quand il parlait de démocratie,
Voici ce qu'il disait :
Il disait :

« Tout comme je ne voudrais pas être esclave, je ne voudrais pas être maître. Ceci exprime mon idée de la démocratie. Tout ce qui diffère de cela, à mesure de la différence, n'est pas une démocratie. »

Abraham Lincoln, seizième président des Etats-Unis, est pour toujours vivant dans la mémoire de ses compatriotes.
Car, sur le champ de bataille de Gettysburg, voici ce qu'il a dit :
Il a dit :

« . . . que de ces morts que nous honorons, nous puissions accroître notre dévouement à la cause pour laquelle ils ont donné l'ultime mesure du dévouement : que nous ici présents soyons résolus à ce qu'ils ne soient pas morts en vain ; que cette nation, sous la protection de Dieu, connaisse une nouvelle naissance de la liberté ; et que le gouvernement par le peuple et pour le peuple ne disparaisse pas de la surface de la terre. »

LINCOLN PORTRAIT

SPRECHER:

„Mitbürger, wir können uns der Geschichte nicht entziehen."

Das sagte er,
Das sagte Abraham Lincoln:

„Mitbürger, wir können uns der Geschichte nicht entziehen. Ungeachtet unserer selbst werden wir - der Kongreß und diese Regierung - wohl nie vergessen werden. Ob wir als einzelne bedeutend oder unwichtig sind, keiner von uns kann sich der Verantwortung entziehen. Die Feuerprobe, die wir gerade durchstehen, wird uns in Ehre oder in Schande bis zum Jüngsten Tag begleiten. Wir - auch wir hier - haben die Macht inne und tragen die Verantwortung."

Er wurde in Kentucky geboren, ist in Indiana aufgewachsen und hat in Illinois gelebt.
Und das sagte er:
Das sagte Abraham Lincoln:
Er sagte:

„Die Dogmen einer ruhigen Vergangenheit gelten nicht für die stürmische Gegenwart. Auf dem Weg, den wir verfolgen liegen viele Steine, aber wir müssen uns der Lage gewachsen zeigen. Da unser Fall neu ist, müssen wir auf neue Art und Weise denken und auf neue Art und Weise handeln. Zuerst müssen wir uns von den Fesseln befreien und dann werden wir unser Land retten."

Wenn er aufrecht stand, war er 1.92 m groß.
Und das sagte er:
Er sagte:

„Es ist der ewige Kampf zwischen zwei Prinzipien: richtig und falsch, auf der ganzen Welt . . . Es ist derselbe Geist, der uns sagt: ‚Du plagst Dich ab und arbeitest und verdienst Dein Brot und ich, ich werde es essen.' Gleichgültig in welcher Form es kommt, ob aus dem Munde eines Königs, der danach trachtet, sich über die Menschen seines eigenen Volkes zu erheben und von den Früchten ihrer Arbeit zu leben, oder von einer Menschenrasse als Entschuldigung dafür, eine andere Rasse zu Sklaven zu machen: es ist dasselbe tyrannische Prinzip!"

Lincoln war ein ruhiger Mann.
Abraham Lincoln war ein ruhiger und melancholischer Mann.
Aber wenn er von Demokratie sprach,
Sagte er das:
Er sagte:

„Da ich kein Sklave sein möchte, will ich auch kein Herr sein. So verstehe ich Demokratie. Was immer davon abweicht, weicht im selben Maß von der Demokratie ab."

Abraham Lincoln, 16. Präsident der Vereinigten Staaten von Amerika, ist unvergeßlich im Gedächtnis seiner Landsleute. Denn auf dem Schlachtfeld von Gettysburg sagte er:
Er sagte:

„ . . . mögen wir von diesen ehrwürdigen Toten die volle Hingabe für die Sache, für die sie das Letzte gegeben haben, lernen, mögen wir an dieser Stelle endgültig verkünden, daß diese Toten nicht umsonst gestorben sind; möge diese Nation mit Gottes Hilfe eine neue Geburt der Freiheit erleben; und möge die Herrschaft durch das Volk und für das Volk auf dieser Erde nicht untergehen."

To Andre Kostelanetz

LINCOLN PORTRAIT

AARON COPLAND
(1942)

28

L. P. - 44

38

Fl. II takes Picc. I

41

L. P. - 44

43

L.P.-44

49

L.P.-44

50

52

L. P. - 44

56

The Speaker text reads:
"When standing erect he was six feet four inches tall. And this is what he said:"
"He said:"
""It is the eternal struggle between two principles — right and wrong — throughout the world."
"It is the same spirit that says: 'You toil and work and earn bread —"
"and I'll eat it!'... No matter in what shape it comes,"
"whether from the mouth of a king who seeks to bestride the people of his own nation and live by the fruit of their labor,"
"or from one race of men as an apology for enslaving another race, it is the same tyrannical principal.""

58

59

62

63

260

DANZÓN CUBANO

Instrumentation

Piccolo
2 Flutes (Flute II doubling Piccolo II)
2 Oboes
Cor Anglais
2 Clarinets in B♭
Bass Clarinet in B♭
2 Bassoons
Contrabassoon
4 Horns in F
3 Trumpets in B♭
3 Trombones
Tuba
Timpani
Xylophone
Percussion
wood block, slap stick, cymbals, snare drum, cow bell, gourd,
Chinese temple blocks, maracas, claves, bass drum
Piano
Strings

Aaron Copland working by candlelight
Photo: Victor Kraft

DANZÓN CUBANO

Moderately (*nonchalant, but precise*) (♩ = 80)

AARON COPLAND

B. & H. 15895

71

B.&H.15895

40
Picc.
I
Flts.
II
Solo
mp
Obs.I.II
Soli a 2
C.A.
Clts.I.II in B♭
a 2
Bass Clt. in B♭
mf
Bsns.I.II
mf stacc.
f
I.II
Hns.in F
III.IV
I
Tpts.in B♭
II.III
stacc.
ff
Trombs.I.II
Tromb.III & Tuba
Cow Bell (Flattened)
struck with metal stick
Gourd
Piano
Vln.I
Vln.II
Vla.
'Cello
Bass
stacc.
mp

B. & H. 15895

B. & H. 15895

83

B.& H.15895

93

B.& H. 15895

B. & H. 15895

B.& H. 15895

99

B. & H. 15895

CLARINET CONCERTO

Instrumentation

Solo Clarinet in B♭
Piano
Harp
Strings

Duration: c. 17½ minutes

CONCERTO FOR CLARINET

and String Orchestra, with Harp and Piano

AARON COPLAND
(1948)

115

B & H 17942

117

B & H 17942

118

In order to allow the soloist some respite before the beginning of the cadenza, the soloist may pause after bar 114 and the harp play the passage in small notes while the strings sustain the chord. A still longer respite may be provided by one solo viola playing the clarinet passage from bar 112, 3rd beat.

B & H 17942

126

130

131

133

B & H 17942

135

B & H 17942

148

152

B & H 17942

154

AARON COPLAND
THREE LATIN-AMERICAN SKETCHES

THREE LATIN-AMERICAN SKETCHES

Contents

Instrumentation

Flute (doubling Piccolo)
Oboe
Clarinet in B♭
Bassoon
Trumpet in C
Piano I
Piano II (*ad lib.*)
Percussion
claves, wood block, xylophone, ratchet, slap stick,
triangle, conga drum, suspended cymbal
Strings
(minimum: 6, 4, 3, 2, 1)

Duration: c. 10 minutes

1. Estribillo

AARON COPLAND

164

B.& H.20262

168

174

B.& H.20262

B.& H.20262

Aug. 31, 1971

2. Paisaje Mexicano

3. Danza de Jalisco

* If conductor prefers, a second percussion player may substitute a slap-stick, in which case the pianists need not "clap hands"

188

190

B.& H.20262

192

B.& H.20262

194

B.& H.20262

195

213

B.& H.20262

214

B.& H.20262